SOCIAL MEDIA CAREER BUILDING™

20 GREAT CAREER-BUILDING ACTIVITIES USING YOUTUBE®

ADAM FURGANG

ROSEN PUBLISHING®
New York

For Caleb and Ben

Published in 2017 by The Rosen Publishing Group, Inc.
29 East 21st Street, New York, NY 10010

First Edition

Library of Congress Cataloging-in-Publication Data

Names: Furgang, Adam, author.
Title: 20 great career-building activities using YouTube / Adam Furgang.
Other titles: Twenty great career-building activities using YouTube
Description: First edition. | New York : Rosen Publishing, 2017. | Series: Social media career building | Audience: Grades 7 to 12. | Includes bibliographical references and index.
Identifiers: LCCN 2016018108 | ISBN 9781508172642 (library bound)
Subjects: LCSH: YouTube (Firm)—Juvenile literature. | Online social networks—Juvenile literature. | Career development—Juvenile literature.
Classification: LCC TK5105.8868.Y68 F87 2017 | DDC 302.30285—dc23
LC record available at https://lccn.loc.gov/2016018108

Manufactured in China

CONTENTS

INTRODUCTION

In 1968, the pop artist Andy Warhol coined the now-famous phrase, "In the future everyone will be famous for 15 minutes." Today the default time limit for videos uploaded to the online video sharing service YouTube is 15 minutes, and anyone who has a YouTube account can share his or her videos for friends, family, or the entire world to see.

Three former employees of online payment service PayPal, Chad Hurley, Steve Chen, and Jawed Karim, launched YouTube in May 2005 as a way for internet users to share videos easily, privately or publicly. At the time, the company was based out of Hurley's garage in Menlo Park, California. Not long after launching YouTube, the popularity of the service grew very quickly as viewers began sharing videos. Many early users of the platform shared videos hosted on YouTube on social networking sites such as MySpace. In October 2006 it was made public that Google was buying YouTube for $1.65 billion in stock.

By 2007, YouTube was already in demand by many international users. Google's popularity helped when launching local YouTube sites in many countries, such as France, Italy, Japan,

From left to right, YouTube cofounders Steve Chen, as chief technology officer, Chad Hurley, as chief executive officer, and Jawed Karim, who uploaded the company's first video, pose in their San Mateo, California, office in 2005.

Spain, and England. According to a YouTube press release in 2016, YouTube has local websites in more than eighty-eight countries, with 80 percent of all viewing coming from outside the United States.

As claimed by the BBC, children today between the ages of seven and sixteen spend more time online than they do watching traditional television programs. Among young people between the ages of fifteen and seventeen, the gap is even more pronounced—with more than three quarters of them typically watching YouTube or other video-on-demand services rather than watching traditional broadcast television.

According to statistics on YouTube's website, "YouTube has over a billion users—almost a third of all people on the Internet—and every day people watch hundreds of millions of hours of YouTube videos and generate billions of views." In addition, YouTube's website states: "YouTube overall, and even YouTube on mobile alone, reaches more 18–34 and 18–49 year-olds than any cable network in the U.S." According to CNN, people watch more than six billion hours of YouTube videos per month.

Users of YouTube around the world can search for almost anything. Videos about news, pop culture television shows, how-to videos, music videos, movie trailers, political or historic speeches, sports events both current and historic, and even some full-length movies are available for free viewing. Often short advertising clips will precede the videos to help YouTube generate revenue.

Even celebrities such as Justin Bieber used YouTube early on to promote themselves and their first work. Start-ups and established companies alike use YouTube to announce and promote new and upcoming products. Apple and Coca-Cola both have YouTube channels to help promote both their products and brand. With YouTube as the more popular alternative to traditional TV viewing for many of today's young people, YouTube stars are often more popular than mainstream celebrities.

YouTube has become more than just an internet-based alternative source for teens to find pop culture and media content. Tech-savvy teens today can use YouTube to help empower their personal creative endeavors, artistic expression, school-related projects, college applications, job prospects, personal development, self-promotion, and a variety of portfolio-building activities.

As YouTube has grown, so have the many alternative and creative uses teens have embraced. You, too, can use YouTube in a positive and creative way to expand your digital communication and literacy skills, discover who you are, and forge a path in life. You may even be the next person to invent new uses for YouTube that have yet to be imagined or discovered.

CHAPTER ONE

Getting to Know YouTube

Even if you have never made a video or used YouTube before, do not let that deter you. YouTube is very easy to use and it is not even necessary to use it on a home computer. You don't even need professional video equipment to shoot videos and upload them to YouTube. People can use Android and iPhone smartphones and tablets to shoot videos, edit them with apps, and then upload them to YouTube. They can even edit videos on the YouTube website with simple editing tools that are provided by the platform.

Before tackling your exciting portfolio-building projects and uploading completed videos to your YouTube account, you will want to first take some time to do tests to get to know the YouTube platform, your mobile device, and your video equipment. The controls for using YouTube are slightly different on a web browser than they are on the YouTube app for a mobile device. Take some time to familiarize yourself with the version of YouTube that works best for you.

For example, if you have only a mobile phone, you will want to download the YouTube app for the device you are using.

MAKING A YOUTUBE ACCOUNT

Before you get started watching, shooting, and uploading videos, you will need to create a YouTube account. Google owns YouTube, and the company makes it very simple to create one Google account that will then give users easy access to the many Google platforms such as Gmail, Google+, and YouTube. You can download the YouTube app for your mobile device and create a new account there, or go to https://accounts.google.com to create a new account on your home computer. When prompted, you will need to enter your first and last name, a username, password, mobile phone number, and other personal information. Be sure to ask an adult for help and permission before you start.

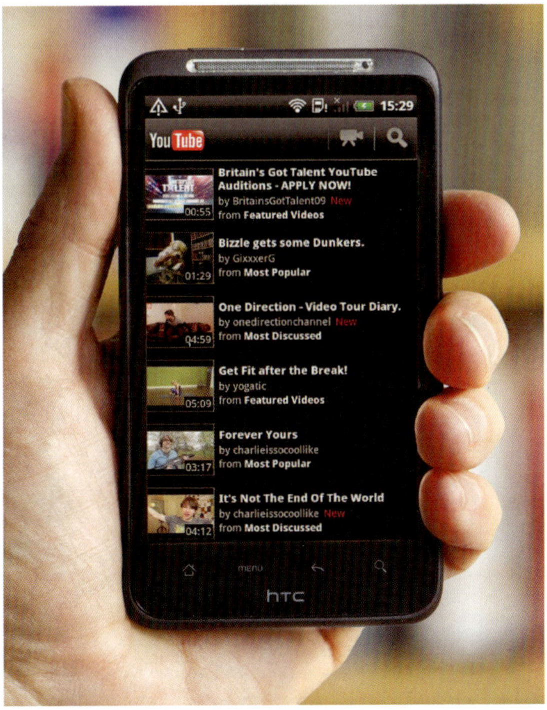

Users can gain access to YouTube on a variety of smartphones using a downloadable mobile app.

Understanding the ins and outs of your home and mobile phones' internet access plan is important before you get started. Mobile phones all have different data plans to access the internet remotely, and you may be charged usage fees for watching and uploading videos to YouTube. Accessing home or public Wi-Fi networks with your mobile device can be a good way to avoid data charges when using YouTube. If you access a public Wi-Fi network, however, do not access private information or enter personal passwords. Hackers can easily gain control of these Wi-Fi networks and steal sensitive information from users in public.

GETTING YOUR FEET WET

Familiarize yourself with the video equipment you own or have access to by shooting some test videos of family or friends. Because videos are moving images, remember to shoot motion to make your videos interesting to watch. Anything that moves can become a good test subject when learning how to use your video equipment. Try shooting a video of a friend riding a bike or maybe a pet running around.

A good tip to remember when shooting video is to hold cell phones and mobile devices the long way—or horizontally. Video shot horizontally will completely fill a computer or TV screen when being played back. Even though it can be done, it's not an advisable idea to hold a mobile phone vertically when shooting video because it will play back as a vertical bar on a computer or TV. A lot of space will be wasted on the sides of the image frame and the picture will not be as close up or easy to watch as a horizontal

Videos you shoot can be transferred to a personal computer and then uploaded to YouTube.

view. Be sure to make some tests yourself so you can see the difference.

If you are filming a nonmoving subject, you can move your camera to create movement. Panning across a landscape and zooming in on a far away building are both good examples of how to create camera motion. Remember to hold steady as you shoot so that your footage is smooth and not jumpy. Attaching your video camera or mobile device to a tripod can help to keep the shots steady.

Another option for filming a nonmoving subject is to take multiple shots of the same thing that can then be edited together later. This alternative can help add variety to your videos. An example of editing would be shooting different angles of two friends playing a game. Eventually you can use an app or software to edit the different shots together in the sequence that you would like to show them.

DIGITAL FOOTPRINT

All of your activities online, including everything you post or upload, contribute to what is called a digital footprint. Think of this footprint as an electronic trace of yourself that exists on the internet. Depending on how you share blogs, photos, and videos, your friends, family, or the public will be able to see what you have posted, long after you have done so. Videos you share privately with friends and assume no one else will see can still be passed along without your permission. It is important to make sure the privacy settings on YouTube are set the way you want them. This step ensures that a video you want only a few friends to see is not visible to the entire world.

It is also important to remember never to share any videos that could be embarrassing, hurtful, or upsetting to others. A silly video of yourself or a friend may seem funny and harmless now, but in only a few short years you may be applying to colleges or filling out online job applications, and that goofy video can become an embarrassment under more professional circumstances. Many prospective employers research job candidates online. It is therefore important to carefully reflect on what videos

CITIZEN TO CELEBRITY VIA YOUTUBE

Because YouTube is open to everyone, anyone with talent, drive, and aspirations has an equal chance of being seen and noticed on the video-sharing service. The public sharing of personal talents on YouTube is an entirely new platform that many people now use to launch themselves into the world of fame and stardom.

In 2009, before the Canadian-born pop singer Justin Bieber had released his first album, *My World,* his online YouTube videos had already been viewed millions of times. His mother had first posted videos of him to YouTube after he came in second at a local singing competition. Today he's one of the most famous pop singers in the world, with well over twenty-five million albums sold worldwide.

More recently, YouTube users, or YouTubers, as they are called, have been able to launch unconventional careers based on the popularity of YouTube videos. Preteens and teens have helped start a new category of celebrity. For example, Jordan Maron, otherwise known by his YouTube username CaptainSparklez, has gotten more than 1.7 billion views of himself and others playing the popular game Minecraft. Through advertising revenue generated by his channel's popularity, the star was able to buy a large mansion that is located in California's Hollywood Hills in 2015.

Jordan Maron, also known as CaptainSparklez, became well known for playing Minecraft on YouTube.

you will be sharing. Making a few judicious decisions now can go a long way toward keeping a positive professional digital footprint for years to come.

EXAMPLES OF DOS AND DON'TS

Before uploading videos to YouTube, make certain that you understand the dos and don'ts of posting online.

- Don't upload everything you record. Stop to consider how others will receive your videos. If you capture some video footage of a friend slipping while ice-skating, for example, it might be amusing to watch together. However, think about whether it is appropriate for everyone to see.
- Do carefully watch your videos before rushing to upload them for all to look at. Some extra time spent viewing, editing, and crafting a video will allow you to spot and remove negative or inappropriate footage. Your goal should be to create the most professional and mature content possible.
- Don't be afraid to learn as you go. You might see many professional YouTube videos that could lead you to be discouraged about your own progress. Remember that the many skills needed for writing, photography, sound, editing, and computer use all come together to make a great YouTube video. Don't expect to be an expert at everything all at once. Once you have a couple of completed videos under your belt you will be able to look back and find mistakes. You can then learn from these mistakes

and improve on your work in future uploads.

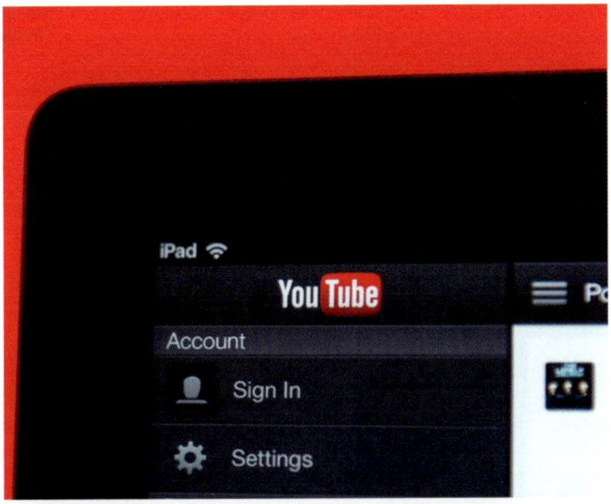

Once you have created an account on a mobile app, you can upload videos directly to YouTube when you shoot videos remotely.

UPLOADING A VIDEO

Now that you have created your own YouTube account, downloaded the app, and produced some video footage, it's time to finally upload a test video to YouTube.

If you have not already done so, download the YouTube app from the app store on your mobile device. Once the app has been downloaded you will want to log into YouTube with your email address and password. After you are in the app, you can easily share videos to your YouTube channel directly from your mobile device.

If you want to use your home computer to upload the videos to YouTube you will need to transfer the videos from your camera or mobile device to your computer first. Depending on your equipment, transferring videos can be done in multiple ways. Make sure you are familiar with the specifics of your computer and video equipment before transferring videos from a video device to a computer.

CHAPTER TWO

How All Teens Can Use YouTube

Deciding what creative endeavor or profession to choose can be a very challenging decision. Although some people are very focused on one specific interest, such as science, sports, dance, acting, music, or art, other people may be unsure of what specifically they want to do or where they are headed in terms of a career. This lack of certainty is not at all uncommon. Everyone has interests, and what they enjoy doing, their hobbies, or even what subjects they excel at in school can all serve to help focus their goals, be they what to major in or what profession to pursue.

YouTube can be used as a tool to help focus interests, build a portfolio, or explore a potential career. Even before you are exactly sure about what direction you want to move in and how YouTube might be beneficial, you can use the video-sharing service in a variety of ways to get you thinking about your interests and your future. Adding new videos to your channel and exploring the vast diversity of content on YouTube can be helpful places to start.

RESEARCH CONTENT PATTERNS

According to statistical data listed on YouTube, "The number of people watching YouTube per day is up 40 percent year over year since March 2014." Other data points to the fact that more than 75 percent of teens between the ages of fifteen and sixteen watch YouTube or other online on-demand services, rather than watching TV programs as they are broadcast. Passively watching video content online has become very popular, and many teens today watch YouTube more than traditional cable television. Becoming focused and exploring professional content can help to broaden your knowledge of the world around you.

News organizations that were traditionally print mediums in the past now have their own YouTube channels. All of the top US newspapers today have companion YouTube channels that post original video news content online. the *New York Times, USA Today,* the *Wall Street Journal,* and the *Washington Post* are just several of the many traditional newspapers that have companion YouTube channels that can be explored for news and creative content. They also provide examples of how YouTube is being employed to supplement and sometimes replace traditional print media. Use the search field at the top of the YouTube homepage to see what news organizations you can find to explore.

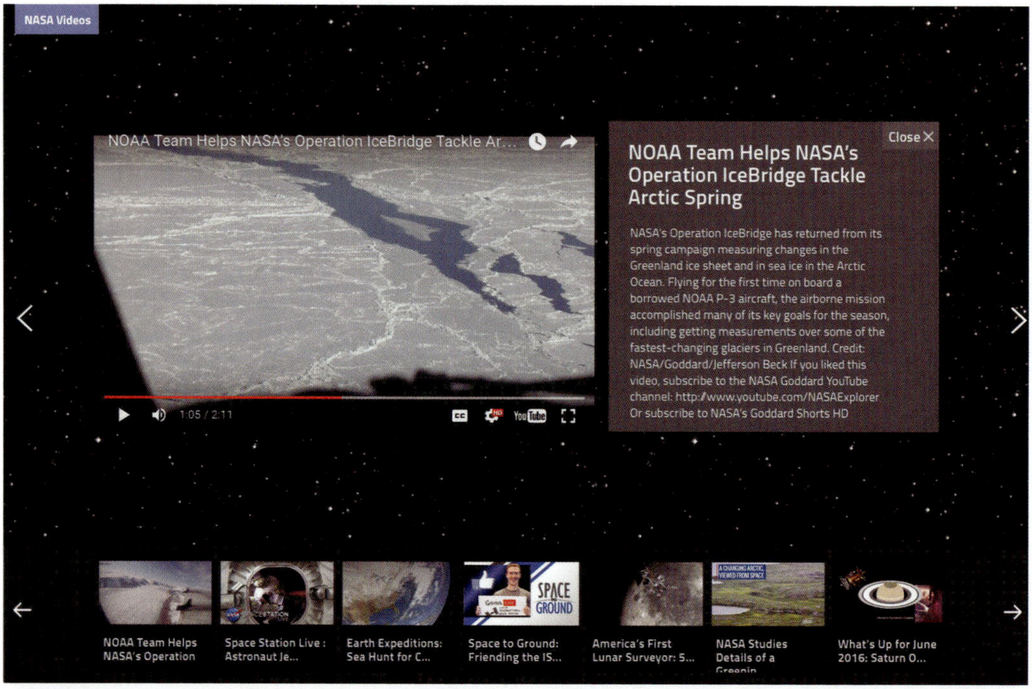

Organizations such as NASA have their own YouTube channels that provide informative videos that can aid students in doing their research.

Today even celebrities, corporations, government departments, and public places have their own YouTube channels. For example, the Grand Canyon National Park, Dunkin' Donuts, *Star Wars*, Target, the National Aeronautics and Space Administration (NASA), the White House, the Walt Disney Company, the National Football League (NFL), Taylor Swift, the US Department of Transportation's National Highway Traffic Safety Administration, The US Mint, and Toys "R" Us all have their own YouTube channels. Searching for YouTube channels will yield some very surprising results and can help spark ideas for how to use YouTube creatively to communicate information as you grow and focus your interests.

Create a list of ten corporate channels to track over a week or two. Make a chart and record the topics of their main posts. Then review your chart and categorize them. Were they mainly news, advertisements, or novelty features? How many views did each video get? What kinds of comments did they receive? Finding these specific patterns can help focus your own channel and assist in understanding what people are responding to online.

BRAND YOUR CHANNEL

Everyone with a YouTube account automatically has a YouTube channel, but there are steps that can be taken to adjust the look and feel of the channel to help build a brand aimed at a goal or profession.

A good first step in branding your YouTube channel is to generate a banner image, a graphic, or art that displays inside the horizontal channel header. Click the pencil icon to "Edit channel art." From there you will be brought to a screen where you can upload photos. At the bottom is a link: "How to create channel art" where more in-depth instructions can be found that will explain a suggested banner dimension, minimum and maximum widths, and a safe area where text will display, no matter what device someone views your channel on. You will also

YOUTUBE KIDS APP

It's important to know that children under the age of thirteen are not allowed to set up a YouTube account. With traditional television viewing steadily declining in the two- to eleven-year-old age range, YouTube has released a kid-friendly app called YouTube Kids for Android and iPhone users. The new service was announced in February 2016 and is designed to help children search online for videos and to avoid inappropriate content.

The content available on the YouTube Kids app is specifically organized for kids with family oriented and educational content in mind. The app's interface and design appeals to young users and allows searches based on age range. Parents or adults can flag any inappropriate content that may find its way onto the service, and the search feature can even be turned off to keep kids from searching without adult help. A time limit can also be set to prevent kids from spending too much time using the app. Once content has been watched, the app suggests similar videos based on what has already been viewed.

If you have a younger sibling or children that you babysit, try creating kid-friendly content for them to watch on the app. Videos that show you singing the alphabet, a song, or simple games such as peek-a-boo are a few ideas that could help you create fun or educational content for a younger audience.

Content generated by students who are younger than thirteen years old can be posted to the YouTube Kids app.

be able to find a link to download the official YouTube Channel Art Templates. These templates are different file formats that can be opened in a photo-editing program such as Photoshop where images, graphics, and text can be added and arranged to create a banner that reflects your channel's focus.

For example, if you are a dancer, a photo of a dance studio could be a good choice for a banner image. It can help to communicate immediately the type of content that will be found on your page.

If your channel will mainly be displaying your art or content related to the art field, then a collage of several of your pieces of art, along with your name or signature, could be a nice banner to display.

If you do not have an image-editing program such as Photoshop on your personal computer, try the art or graphics department at your school to ask if one is available. Another good solution is to download a free trial of the program from the internet or use the free Google photo-editing program Picasa. Apple computers come with a photo-editing application called iPhoto, which can work for cropping and adjusting photos.

RECORD YOUR OWN LIFE

Now that you have explored the extensive variety of content on YouTube it's time to record your own life and begin to share some focused content.

No matter what your interests are, you can record videos of yourself and share them to help build a small following of friends and family while getting to learn the ins and outs of YouTube. Here are a few ideas to help get you going on your way to posting some videos:

- Set up a tripod and record yourself playing a musical instrument or start a band with friends. After you have a few videos, send an email to friends and family members announcing your new home-brewed music channel.
- Make a time-lapse video of yourself as you draw or paint a picture. Many new mobile phones today allow users to record slow motion or time-lapse video. These effects can contribute to making your videos more dynamic.
- Record yourself giving a video review of new music, films, television shows, or video games. Remember to make it personal and unique. Your best asset is your individual point of view and the way you see the world.
- Record yourself performing a sports activity. Dancing, skating, and shooting baskets are just a few activities you can easily film yourself doing with a camera and a tripod.

RECORD YOUR WORLD

Not everyone with a YouTube channel needs to create original content about themselves to put up online. Many professionals such as news reporters and journalists shoot videos about events in the world around them. Your friends, family, school, and community can all be used as subjects for a YouTube channel.

You can work with your friends, school peers, and members of your community to generate exclusive news content for your YouTube channel.

- Film a sibling's birthday party or event and edit it together. Once it is posted online everyone who attended the event can view it with a link to the channel or video.
- Interview an older person about his or her life. Ask the kinds of questions that someone your age might be concerned with or curious about.
- Set up a time-lapse video of a building, weather event, or even your kitchen during dinnertime. Research online how to take and edit time-lapse videos. They can provide a fun perspective on your daily life.

Use YouTube to document your crafts and hobbies as you learn them. Filming computer repair skills, for example, can be uploaded to promote your talents and begin enhancing your academic digital footprint.

LEARN A NEW CRAFT

Learning can be fun and entertaining at the same time. Even if you have not mastered a skill, make videos of yourself as you progress. Recording the learning process can be valuable to you as well as your audience. Sometimes people learn more from seeing their mistakes than from seeing something done correctly every time.

Cooking shows are very popular on YouTube, and anyone can start one. For example, the CharlisCrafty-Kitchen channel on YouTube features two young girls making desserts and treats. The channel has been viewed more than 285 million times. Don't be afraid to take the plunge and film yourself and a friend or a sibling having fun, being silly, and learning as you go. A few examples of new crafts or skills to film are the following:

- sewing
- gardening
- playing a video game
- woodworking
- yoga or martial arts

There's a lot to explore on YouTube. Why not have your explorations benefit your career and interest goals?

CHAPTER THREE

YouTube for Education

Though many people go to YouTube for entertainment purposes, education is also a large and growing aspect of the video-sharing service. In 2004, American businessman Salman Khan started tutoring his cousin in math. After getting more tutoring requests, Khan decided to record his short lectures and post them on YouTube. By 2006, he had started the free educational video service Khan Academy. In 2012, Khan was named one of the one hundred most influential people by *Time* magazine. As of 2015, Khan Academy has 2.2 million YouTube subscribers and 440 million free micro-lectures, according to Forbes.com. The videos have been viewed more then 762 million times.

There are many ways to use YouTube for educational purposes beyond just teaching. For example, you can create YouTube videos to help apply for college, present strong reports for school, promote your school, or report about school issues, clubs, and after school activities. Remember, education can be fun beyond the classroom, and any content you create can help you build a portfolio or even a career.

Explore some of the most popular educational YouTube channels to see what they offer. There are channels for learners of all ages. For example, check out channels such as TEDx Talks, Crash-Course, and Khan Academy. There are also many good channels for young people who wish to go into the primary education field, such as Sesame Street or LittleBabyBum.

Salman Khan, founder of the educational YouTube channel Khan Academy, provides videos for all levels of learning.

FUND-RAISING VIDEOS

Fund-raisers can be very beneficial to schools by generating much-needed money for new technology, equipment, class trips, repairs, improvements, or assistance for families in need. Creating a series of videos with the objective of fund-raising can be an effective way to showcase your school and convey that you are civic-minded.

Before a fund-raiser has occurred, you can make a video that concentrates on the details surrounding the fund-raiser, such as where and when it will be held, as well as what the specific goals of the fund-raiser are. Hand-drawn titles for your video can give it a homemade feel. If a more professional look is required, titles can be generated in image-editing applications. Be sure to get the announcement video up onto your YouTube channel well in advance of the event so that you can send out links to the video for promotional purposes. When the fund-raiser occurs, you can film

Use YouTube to share videos of your fund-raising activities to help promote your group or organization.

the event and edit the highlights together into a video before you post it. Then include a follow-up video to list the goals that were achieved and to thank the people who were involved. This three-video approach can even provide the event with the attention it deserves.

Remember not to focus on only your own friends and family in the videos. Try to include teachers, faculty members, and as many people as you can in the videos so that they represent the entire group or community involved in the fund-raiser. If long-term goals are achieved with the fund-raiser, you might continue your documentary efforts. For example, if funds were generated with the aim that everyone can go on a class trip to a museum, a video can be made of that trip and then added to the YouTube channel. Several videos showcasing a concrete beginning, middle, and end will help future fund-raisers by allowing people to see the results of a collective effort.

A YOUTUBE CHANNEL FOR THE CLASSROOM

Some teachers run their own YouTube channels and require student participation for the channel to be successful throughout the school year. Express your interest to your teacher if you'd like to take part and help out. If no such school channel exists, try making one on your own. You can document lessons or teacher demonstrations over time. Weekly or monthly news updates can be produced in the form of short informative videos that describe the topics covered, test dates, and upcoming events such as class trips or projects.

Once a teacher agrees to the creation of the channel, goals can be laid out for what will be filmed, when, and how often videos can be uploaded. Getting ideas from a teacher can be very helpful and the teacher might be able to provide access to equipment that can be used for the production. If you cannot get permission from the teacher and students to film the class, try filming an after-school activity that does not interfere with a teacher's classroom.

A group of friends can also work together to create a classroom channel that serves as a study aid. Topics discussed in class can be revisited in the form of short informative videos created during study sessions.

Another classroom channel could focus on an elective class in which student projects or performances are filmed and displayed online for everyone to see. Art, music, dance, computer, and even video electives are all great subjects to document for an ongoing YouTube channel.

RECORD ORAL PRESENTATIONS

With permission from your teacher, you can present school reports or projects using YouTube videos. A book report, science essay, or social studies report

Briarcrest Christian High School students in Memphis, Tennessee, shared their award ceremony on YouTube to show that they won $25,000 in a singing competition.

can all be written out and researched in the traditional way, then filmed to create a short presentation. You can set up a tripod and record yourself speaking as you read. Hold up visuals during your report or edit them in later.

Another way to present a video of a report is to film various elements such as the book you are reporting on, pictures from that book, and images of the author and

HOW TO USE GOPRO CAMERAS

If you are interested in getting video equipment to produce dynamic footage beyond what a mobile phone is capable of, a GoPro video camera might be helpful. GoPro makes small, versatile, and mountable video cameras that create wide-angle, high-definition still images and videos. Special effects such as time-lapse video can also be achieved with GoPro cameras. Special attachments allow GoPro cameras to be attached to many unusual places such as bikes, cars, skateboards, and even the top of your head on a helmet. For example, to film a video of yourself skiing, you could wear a GoPro camera on your helmet or chest and ski down a mountain, capturing professional quality, high-definition video as you go.

GoPro cameras are often mounted on high-flying drones because they are so lightweight and are able to get aerial shots that would otherwise be impracticable or impossible to capture.

GoPro sells both entry-level and performance-level cameras with a variety of features and functions. The different models of cameras are all fairly simple to use, and the recorded footage can be downloaded to a computer or even on your mobile phone with the use of a GoPro app. Video footage can also be accessed and edited on a free GoPro desktop app. If the cost of acquiring a brand new GoPro camera is outside your budget, you can still find used models for sale on eBay with the help of an adult. Check out the GoPro YouTube channel or website for examples of videos and listings of the cameras, instructions, and the typical uses of each.

related material. A voiceover of you speaking the report can be added after all elements are filmed and edited together. Art and music can be added if needed. If your teacher requires a traditional written report, a separate video can be made and presented for extra credit.

As a long-term goal, consider putting together a small video library of your presentations to showcase your work over the course of a semester or school year. A YouTube channel that collects your projects all in one place can be a nice link to provide to the colleges you are applying to. It can also be presented to someone hiring for summer internships related to school or specific school subjects.

IMPRESS A COLLEGE RECRUITER

For many students, applying to colleges can be stressful and intimidating. If you have a specific talent or ability that you wish to explore in college, showcasing that talent on a YouTube channel can be an excellent opportunity to get the attention of college recruiters. If you are applying to an art school for drawing, painting, sculpture, or photography, for example, a YouTube channel that focuses on your work and skills is a good way to get attention and be remembered. Even science experiments, school debates, or oral presentations of creative writing are excellent events to record for recruiters.

Take short videos or pictures of your work, and create a focused YouTube channel that can be viewed easily with or without sound. Adding a bold title with

Keep a video history of your growing talents on YouTube to showcase your work to college recruiters. These teens are making videos that use Claymation, animation featuring clay figures.

your full name and picture at the beginning will help recruiters to remember you and your projects.

Prospective art students have an especially good opportunity to showcase their work on YouTube. Post short videos of your artwork, and add the title and year to the video title. Adding the title and year to the post can serve as a way to catalog your work. If you are making videos of your art, be sure to hold the camera steady or use a tripod. If you are presenting sculpture, remember to circle around the work so it can be seen from all sides.

MAKE A PERSONAL TRAILER

An engaging portfolio piece to help you stand out from the crowd can be to create a fake movie trailer of your life, showcasing what you have accomplished. Include a "Coming Soon" section to highlight your budding abilities and long-term goals. Add titles or dramatic voiceovers that emphasize important schoolwork, accomplishments, and goals.

Whether you are applying to college for a major in sports, math, English, or any other subject, you can approach the process with creativity and fun. A memorable trailer can stay in the mind of a recruiter or college application reviewer for a long time to come.

Whether the activities you try benefit your educational pursuits directly or simply help you practice using YouTube creatively, these activities can help you build a positive digital footprint online.

CHAPTER FOUR

YouTube for Creative Endeavors

Promoting creative endeavors, building a portfolio, and showcasing career-oriented activities on YouTube are useful ways to focus your talent. If you are an illustrator, graphic designer, fine artist, or photographer, you can compile still images of your work into a video portfolio to send to college recruiters or potential employers. Music videos, short films, acting, dancing, and cooking can all be documented in short videos for your YouTube channel.

Going to YouTube and using the search feature at the top of the home page to look for examples of what others have posted within your specific area of interest is a great place to get started. Once you see what other people are doing you can start brainstorming fresh ideas of your own for an engaging YouTube channel to highlight your creative skills.

MAKE YOUR OWN CREATIVE VIDEO

With the help of some friends or even the use of a tripod-mounted video camera, you can shoot your own imaginative production and then edit it before posting it on YouTube. The performing arts such as dancing, acting, and singing are especially good subjects for these endeavors.

Shoot the performance with several mobile phones or video cameras so you can see the presentation from

These students use a tripod-mounted camera to capture a school performance on video.

different angles. The footage can then be edited together later, giving you a variety of angles and takes so the resulting video does not consist of one long static shot.

You can even make fliers or posters for the performance so that you can have an audience to record. A well-documented and nicely edited video that also features your talents can be an important addition to any YouTube channel. As you work, keep your long-term goals in mind as well—gaining YouTube subscribers, helping your application to colleges, or standing out to employers in your field of interest.

MAKE A DOCUMENTARY

If you're interested in history, writing, journalism, filmmaking, photography, or sportscasting, then creating a short documentary can be a good way to get practice learning what these fields might be like. Carefully research the topic or area of study and approach it as you would a report. Collect photos, news articles, interviews, and even video clips. Documentaries can be made to simply inform the audience about a

These high school seniors have involved local community members at the historical society as they make a documentary about their hometown.

topic or issue, or they can be used to persuade the audience to agree with a certain point of view about a topic or issue.

If you are using existing copyrighted material in your documentary, be sure to use it only in a limited capacity and always credit the source material. Fair use laws permit the use of copyrighted material for filmed commentary or criticisms, such as in film reviews. They can also be used in comedic parodies. News segments on late night talk shows are good examples of fair use in which copyrighted products, television shows, films, or literature can be used humorously.

MAKE A REALITY SHOW OF YOUR LIFE

Reality shows have been one of the most popular television formats for years. Creating a reality show of your own life is fun, and it is also a way to showcase your skills and talents simultaneously. Show how you can be a writer, director, actor, and creative director all at one time. Ask someone to film you all day long as you go about doing a specific creative task. Showcase the process you go through so that prospective schools or employers can see your creative method. Create short interviews to intersperse between the edited scenes in which you talk about the project. Interview friends or family members, and include those interviews as well.

Be playful and entertaining, but remember to keep the overall focus on your skill or talent so that after a few episodes are online they will serve as different aspects of a growing portfolio of your work or skill.

UNBOX A PRODUCT

In recent years, a new YouTube video phenomenon called "unboxing" has developed. Unboxing is when a person gets a new product or gadget on or before its first day on the market, then that person videotapes and describes the product as he or she opens it. The resulting video is next uploaded to YouTube. Online viewers then get to see exactly what they will experience if they purchase the item themselves. Because of how popular these videos are, some companies are even filming their own unboxing of their products that they post on their official YouTube company channel. For example, Microsoft's YouTube channel has an unboxing of the Xbox One that has been viewed more than three million times.

You could make your own unboxing video for a personal creation or just film the unboxing of a new product, gadget, or acquisition to share with your YouTube followers. Filming your own unboxing videos and posting them to YouTube is a great way to meet followers with similar interests, as well as promote your interests. For example, if your YouTube channel focuses on your goals as a musician, then an unboxing video of new headphones, an instrument, or speakers would be an interesting addition to your YouTube channel.

Evan of the YouTube channel EvanTubeHD unboxes a LEGO Star Wars Millennium Falcon building kit on the TV show *Good Morning America*. Unboxing new products became popular on YouTube.

YOUTUBE SETTINGS AND ADVANCED FEATURES

As you become more familiar with YouTube you can begin to explore some of the platform's more advanced features. Clicking the gear icon below your channel header will open the channel setting dialogue box where privacy, account setting, layout customization, and advanced settings are all available.

Privacy and account settings will allow you to make your videos and subscriptions private or public. To customize the layout of your channel, slide the bar from gray to blue. Once active, you will be able to control what visitors see when they view your channel. Next, follow the instructions to make your own channel trailer. You can also create channel sections to help you control the look of your channel.

Enabling the monetization feature on YouTube will allow ads to be displayed alongside your videos. Be sure to follow the guidelines for the monetization process carefully. It involves submitting videos for approval and allowing YouTube to place ads near or inside your video. It also involves opening an account for receiving funds generated through ads, called an AdSense account. Keep in mind that earnings are not dispensed into the account until they reach a certain amount. Become thoroughly aware of all guidelines and get permission from an adult before entering any agreements. Also research any income levels that you may reach that would cause you to be taxed by your state or federal government.

These settings and advanced features are good to stay familiar with as your channel grows and your skills improve.

CROWDSOURCE A PERSONAL PROJECT

Have you ever wondered how some people get the money to make their creative projects? Crowdsourcing is a popular way for people to earn money for creative endeavors. Crowdsourcing means obtaining funding or help for an idea or project from a larger group of people who wish to be involved financially or help out with that project. The term "crowdsourcing" (or "crowdfunding") was coined in 2006 by Jeff Howe of *Wired* magazine as a way to describe the practice that was growing in popularity on the internet. Some of the more popular crowdsourcing websites are Kickstarter.com, indiegogo.com, Crowdfunder.com, and rockethub.com. Each site has its own guidelines for funding or investing in projects.

The most favored Crowdsourcing site is Kickstarter. The website states, "Our mission is to help bring creative projects to life." According to the site, "Kickstarter helps artists, musicians, filmmakers, designers, and other creators find the resources and support they need to make their ideas a reality. To date, tens of thousands of creative projects—big and small—have come to life with the support of the Kickstarter community."

If you have a small project that needs financial backing, Kickstarter is a good place to go for help. Be sure to read through the Kickstarter rules and age requirements so you are familiar with the guidelines before starting a project. Completed projects are shared or distributed to backers, so you would have a

Videos hosted on YouTube are commonly used on KickStarter.com to describe a new product or business endeavor and to foster support for it.

responsibility to your backers, and you must be willing and able to follow through on that responsibility.

Kickstarter has a YouTube page that features interviews, discussions, and videos of projects created through the website. Many Kickstarter projects also use YouTube videos to describe the potential projects, their goals, and what backers will receive upon completion of a project. Be sure to check it out before deciding to embark on generating funds for your own creative undertaking. To get a good sense of the process, it might also be a good idea to consider backing a small project through Kickstarter before starting your own.

CHAPTER FIVE

YouTube for Professional Uses

When YouTube first started, professionals did not post content there. Today, most major companies and corporations have YouTube channels. Even traditional broadcast networks such as NBC, CBS, PBS, CNN, and HBO as well as many of their individual shows have their own YouTube channels. *Sesame Street*, *The Tonight Show Starring Jimmy Fallon*, *Saturday Night Live,* and *The Ellen DeGeneres Show* all have YouTube channels for self-promotion and as a secondary outlet for loyal subscribers who want to catch a missed segment. Many people often share links to clips or funny highlights from a show that aired the previous night. The sharing of links of television clips provides free promotions for shows and helps to draw in more viewers to the show.

Just as entertainment outlets use YouTube for professional purposes, you, too, can use it for self-promotion and to get yourself noticed. There are many professional ways to use the video-sharing site to make yourself known if you are serious about the field.

MAKE A HOW-TO VIDEO

Most people have seen how-to videos on the internet, and many use them to figure out how to do everything from fix a radiator to cook a meal. But what if you were looking for a partner to open a catering business with? A how-to video could really show off your cooking skills. If you wanted to start a landscaping business, a how-to video about trimming hedges or changing the oil in a lawnmower could be used to promote your business and show prospective clients that you know what you're doing.

First Lady Michelle Obama described the Let's Move! campaign to Ellen DeGeneres on the TV show *Ellen*. The video of breaking down the dance moves component became popular on YouTube.

Having someone film you is a good way to showcase your skills and help your personality shine through. Or, using a GoPro camera can assist in filming the video from your own point of view. Consider your intended audience before deciding how you will film the video. Prepare a script ahead of time so that you know the main points you want to make in your video. YouTube channels like eHow, Howcast, and Household-Hacker are all beneficial how-to YouTube channels to visit and investigate for ideas.

MAKE A VISUAL RÉSUMÉ

If you've successfully gotten a start-up business off the ground—even a small one—or if you are just building a portfolio of professional work, making a short commercial or a visual résumé can be a great promotional addition to your YouTube channel.

Gather your best work or videos, and edit together short powerful clips that highlight your strengths. If your business is computer tech support, then show a few shots of yourself at work with a client, along with a few voiceovers or quick clips of clients giving praise for your quality work. This can all be brought together in a short informative commercial. Be sure to give the name of your business or profession at the beginning along with any important contact information at the end.

Even if you don't have a start-up yet you can still create a short visual résumé or commercial of collected works. Be it gardening or computer programming, or sewing new clothing and fixing old cars, each and every interest or budding professional endeavor can be shot on video, edited, and crafted into a portfolio video. A paper résumé that includes a link at the bottom of the page pointing job recruiters or potential bosses to a YouTube video can add to your listed skills and give a personal touch to help you stand out.

START A WEBSITE TO HOST YOUR VIDEOS

Linking your YouTube videos to your personal website can help showcase your skills or promote your business.

Most businesses today have websites that help to draw in new clients or provide a place for existing customers to go for information. Creating a small website and adding YouTube videos from your channel can help the website stand out.

Use YouTube to host your videos of related professional projects. Numerous websites enable YouTube videos to be embedded, so even if you simply start a blog, you can host your YouTube videos from there.

Blogspot.com is a free blogging site that allows YouTube videos to be linked to it. Creating a blog is a terrific way to bring together and promote any informative text, photos, links, and YouTube videos you have worked so hard at crafting.

Depending on your goals for a blog or website, Blogspot.com and other blog services like Tumblr.com have a variety of free templates to choose from so you can have a professional-looking site immediately. Using a similar banner for all of your professional online endeavors will help to brand your company or services. This way the banner for your YouTube channel can be adapted for use in other places on the internet.

VLOG ABOUT YOUR PROFESSIONAL INTERESTS

The word "vlog" is short for "video-blog." Video blogs can take the place of traditional blogs. They can be used for all kinds of purposes, but vlogging about professional topics can help you get ahead in your chosen field and become part of the dialogue about your industry.

Vloggers typically look directly into the camera and speak about their topic from their point of view. If you review new products or media on your vlog, be sure to have the content present so you can show it as you speak, because that's one of the benefits of the format. Vlogs can also cut away to other footage or product close-ups while you are talking. To accomplish this, you will need to film complete video shots in long takes and

Besides writing content for your website, make video logs, or vlogs, to report content.

then separately film other footage of products, clips, close-ups, or cut-aways and edit them together. Many video editing programs enable video and audio clips to be separated after the fact. This process is a good way to keep the audio of you talking while a cutaway of other elements is shown. Be sure to go to YouTube and search for professional vlogs to see how they are edited. Learning a new technique from watching what you already enjoy is an invaluable way to get ideas.

SELL PRODUCTS WITH A YOUTUBE VIDEO

Selling items online is a huge business. In 2015, more than 80 billion dollars worth of merchandise was sold on eBay alone. Online sellers typically describe and photograph items before posting them to sell. Creating a short video of the product being sold and linking it

"TESTED.COM"

The website Tested.com is for industry professionals who use YouTube to showcase their skills doing what they love and appreciate. Tested.com was created by Will Smith and Norman Chan in 2010 "as a place to share their interests and passions with the world." Tested.com videos are hosted by Jamie Hyneman and Adam Savage. Hyneman and Savage also previously hosted the Discovery Channel TV show *MythBusters,* where they put myths, rumors, and urban legends under scrutinizing tests. The site features YouTube videos that showcase fun ways to use technology. In the videos, the hosts build props, puppets, and other models. The site also provides other ways to view exclusive content by paying for a subscription, if desired. This limited subscription method is a great example of how to provide free content and then also monetize or crowd-source content to generate revenue and exclusive content for paid subscribers.

Products such as these 3D-printed mugs can be sold online and accompanied by YouTube videos that document how they were made and display your skills.

to YouTube can enable potential buyers to get a better idea of what they will be buying. If the product is used, then a video of it in close-up can help show that it is in good working condition. Remember to keep your videos short and focused.

Many people like to make and sell their own creations online. If you have original art, crafts, or even 3D-printed objects, you can sell these original creations on many different retail sites. Etsy.com is one site that caters to the makers of handcrafted goods. A personal page can be set up to showcase your products. There you can post descriptions, images, and YouTube videos of what you will be selling. Sending links to pictures or videos of items that you have already sold online is a great way to showcase your skills to colleges or job recruiters. A YouTube video accompanying any item for sale will showcase it better than a still photo is capable of.

If a website will not allow a YouTube video to be embedded on a selling page, it may be possible to include a link to the video that the customer can copy and paste into his or her web browser.

KEEPING UP WITH THE FUTURE

Using YouTube as a pathway to a career or future educational endeavor means that you can take one of the most popular online tools and use it to your advantage. You can either use the tool to consume content or you can make content and allow the tool to work for you.

Be sure to improve your YouTube channel over time so that it keeps pace with advances in your skills. Consider removing old or outdated content and take a serious, focused approach going forward. The best thing to remember is that your YouTube channel should evolve as you do. Keep it fresh!

GLOSSARY

blog A website or web page in a journal format; web log.

crowdsourcing Obtaining funding or other help from a larger group of people.

customize To make something specialized for a particular task.

dialogue box The area on a computer screen where the user is prompted to type or select choices.

digital footprint The trail of data that a person automatically makes and leaves behind when using the internet.

documentary A filmed production about a nonfiction topic, typically including interviews and factual records or reports.

embed To place something inside another entity.

header The top section of a document, before the content starts.

monetization The process of converting into currency.

on-demand Able to be called up or used when needed.

portfolio A collection of related works to display one's skills to an audience such as a potential employer.

remotely From a distance; without being present.

revenue Income.

start-up A newly established business.

template A pre-existing design or format that can be adapted and used repeatedly without being recreated each time.

tripod A three-legged stand for holding a camera steady and in place.

unboxing The process of removing a product from its box while being recorded in a visual format.

vlog A blog that contains mainly videos.

voiceover Narration for a broadcast that is played without the image of the speaker.

FOR MORE INFORMATION

Center for Media Literacy
22837 Pacific Coast Highway, #472
Malibu, CA 90265
(310) 804-3985
Email: cml@medialit.com
Website: http://www.medialit.com
The Center for Media Literacy is an educational organization that provides professional development, public education and resources, and leadership about digital literacy.

Digital Media Association
1050 17th Street NW, Suite 220
Washington, DC 20036
(202) 639-9509
Email: lknife@digmedia.org
Website: http://www.digmedia.org
The Digital Media Association represents the digital media industry and its services and innovators.

International Academy of Digital Arts and Sciences
22 West 21st Street, 7th Floor
New York, NY 10010
(212) 675-4890
Email: seth@iadas.net
Website: http://www.iadas.net
The International Academy of Digital Arts and Sciences is an organization that supports creative, technical, and professional advances in interactive media on the internet.

International Digital Media and Arts Association
101 North College Avenue
Lebanon Valley College
Annville, PA 17003
(423) 794-9996
Email: admin@idmaa.org
Website: http://www.idmaa.org
The International Digital Media and Arts Association is a group formed by fifteen universities interested in teaching and exploring new avenues in the area of digital media.

MediaSmarts: Canada's Centre for Digital and Media Literacy
950 Gladstone Avenue, Suite 120
Ottawa, ON K1Y 3E6
Canada
(613) 224-7721
Email: info@mediasmarts.ca
Website: http://www.mediasmarts.ca
MediaSmarts is an organization dedicated to digital and media literacy for teens, including making wise decisions online.

National Association for Media Literacy Education (NAMLE)
10 Laurel Hill Drive
Cherry Hill, NJ 08003
(888) 775-2652
Email: mciullalipkin@namle.net
Website: http://www.namle.net

NAMLE is an organization that seeks to expand and improve media literacy practices in the United States.

National Film Board of Canada
PO Box 6100
Station Centreville
Montreal, QC H3C-3H5
Canada
(800) 267-7710
Email: https://www.nfb.ca/about/contact-us
Website: https://www.nfb.ca
The National Film Board of Canada is a public agency that makes films and digital content. Its work includes interactive and educational digital media.

WEBSITES

Because of the changing nature of internet links, Rosen Publishing has developed an online list of websites related to the subject of this book. This site is updated regularly. Please use this link to access the list:

http://www.rosenlinks.com/SMCB/you

FOR FURTHER READING

Ascher, Steven, and Edward Pincus. *The Filmmaker's Handbook: A Comprehensive Guide for the Digital Age.* 4th ed. New York, NY: Plume, 2012.

Ciampa, Rob, Theresa Moore, and John Carucci. *YouTube Channels for Dummies.* New York, NY: John Wiley & Sons, 2015

Eckhart, Ann. *How to Start a YouTube Channel for Fun & Profit!* Seattle, WA: Amazon Digital Services, 2014.

Hale, Howard. *The SmartPhone Video Toolkit: The Fastest Way to Create Quality Videos with Your Phone.* Seattle, WA: CreateSpace Independent Publishing Platform, 2015.

Jarboe, Greg. *YouTube and Video Marketing: An Hour a Day.* 2nd ed. Indianapolis, IN: John Wiley & Sons, 2012.

Lanier, Troy, and Clay Nichols. *Filmmaking for Teens: Pulling Off Your Shorts.* 2nd ed. Studio City, CA: Michael Wiese Productions, 2014.

Lastufka, Alan, and Michael W. Dean. *YouTube: An Insider's Guide to Climbing the Charts.* Sebastopol, CA: O'Reilly Media, 2009.

Mariotti, Steve. *The Young Entrepreneur's Guide to Starting and Running a Business: Turn Your Ideas into Money!* New York, NY: Crown Business, 2014.

McKinnon, Andrew. *YouTube: Ultimate YouTube Guide to Building a Channel, Audience and to Start Making Passive Income.* Seattle, WA: CreateSpace Independent Publishing Platform, 2015.

Miles, Jason G. *YouTube Marketing Power: How to Use Video to Find More Prospects, Launch Your Products, and Reach a Massive Audience.* New York, NY: McGraw-Hill Education, 2014.

Myers, Greg F. *YouTube for Beginners: The Complete Guide for Marketing Techniques, Audience Building, & Audience Retention.* Seattle, WA: CreateSpace Independent Publishing Platform, 2015.

Rankin, Kenrya. *Start It Up: The Complete Teen Business Guide to Turning Your Passions into Pay.* San Francisco, CA: Zest Books, 2011.

Rich, Jason. *Ultimate Guide to YouTube for Business.* Irvine, CA: Entrepreneur Press, 2013.

Sharpe, Christopher. *YouTube Black Book: How to Create a Channel, Build an Audience, and Make Money on YouTube.* Ebook. Seattle, WA: Amazon Digital Services, 2014.

BIBLIOGRAPHY

Alba, Davey. "Google Launches 'YouTube Kids,' a New Family-Friendly App." Wired.com, February 23, 2015 (http://www.wired.com/2015/02/youtube-kids).

Coughlan, Sean. "Time Spent Online 'Overtakes TV' Among Youngsters." BBC, January 26, 2016 (http://www.bbc.com/news/education-35399658).

"Fair Use Frequently Asked Questions." TeachingCopyright.org. Retrieved March 8, 2016 (https://www.teachingcopyright.org/handout/fair-use-faq).

Grigoriadis, Vanessa. "Justin Bieber: God, Girls, and Boatloads of Swag." RollingStone.com, March 3, 2011 (http://www.rollingstone.com/music/news/justin-biebers-god-girls-and-boatloads-of-swag-20110303).

Hoffman, Jan. "Justin Bieber Is Living the Dream." NYTimes.com, December 31, 2009 (http://www.nytimes.com/2010/01/03/fashion/03bieber.html).

Howe, Jeff. "The Rise of Crowdsourcing." Wired.com, June 1, 2006 (http://www.wired.com/2006/06/crowds).

Hua, Karen. "Education as Entertainment: YouTube Sensations Teaching the Future." Forbes.com, June 23, 2015 (http://www.forbes.com/sites/karenhua/2015/06/23/education-as-entertainment-youtube-sensations-teaching-the-future/#7e8eda084ca1).

Kelly, Heather. "The Bizarre, Lucrative World of 'Unboxing' Videos." CNN.com, February 13, 2014 (http://www.cnn.com/2014/02/13/tech/web/youtube-unboxing-videos).

Lohr, Steve. "The Crowd Is Wise (When It's Focused)." NYTimes.com, July 18, 2009 (http://www.nytimes.com/2009/07/19/technology/internet/19unboxed.html?_r=0).

Meigs, James B. "What We Owe the MythBusters." NYTimes.com, November 5, 2015 (http://www.nytimes.com/2015/11/05/opinion/what-we-owe-the-mythbusters.html?_r=0).

"Our Rules." Kickstarter.com. Retrieved March 12, 2016 (https://www.kickstarter.com/rules).

"A Personalized Learning Resource for All Ages." KhanAcademy.org. Retrieved March 8, 2016 (https://www.khanacademy.org/about).

Smith, Craig. "By the Numbers: 37 Amazing eBay Statistics." ExpandedRamblings.com, March 12, 2016 (http://expandedramblings.com/index.php/ebay-stats/).

"Statistics." YouTube.com. Retrieved March 2, 2016 (https://www.youtube.com/yt/press/en-GB/statistics.html).

"Teen Safety." YouTube.com. Retrieved March 2, 2016 (https://support.google.com/youtube/answer/2802244?hl=en).

"These Little Kids Make $127,000 on YouTube—PER MONTH." KimKomando.com, April 16, 2015 (http://www.komando.com/happening-now/304414/these-little-kids-make-127000-on-youtube-per-month/all).

"U.S. Copyright Office Fair Use Index." Copyright.gov. Retrieved March 8, 2016 (http://copyright.gov/fair-use).

"Who Is Tested?" Tested.com. Retrieved March 12, 2016 (http://www.tested.com/about/).

INDEX

ABOUT THE AUTHOR

Since he was a teenager, Adam Furgang has created countless home-brewed videos, and now he has his own YouTube channel. He attended the High School of Art and Design and the University of the Arts and has worked as a graphic designer, web designer, fine artist, freelance photographer, and writer. His current writing credits include more than a dozen nonfiction books for middle school readers. He lives in upstate New York with his favorite photo subjects—his wife and two sons.

PHOTO CREDITS

Cover SpeedKingz/Shutterstock.com; p. 3 everything possible/Shutterstock.com; pp. 4–5 background solarseven/Shutterstock.com; pp. 4–5 (inset) © Martin Klimek/ZUMA Press; p. 9 © Ian Dagnall/Alamy Stock Photo; p. 11 Hill Street Studios/Blend Images/Getty Images; p. 13 © Ringo Chiu via ZUMA Wire; p. 15 © iStockphoto.com/dem10; p. 18 NASA; p. 20 The Washington Post/Getty Images; p. 23 Chris Schmidt/E+/Getty Images; p. 24 Hero Images/Getty Images; p. 27 © AP Images; p. 28 Camille Tokerud/The Image Bank/Getty Images; pp. 30–31 Brandon Dill/AP Images for Macy's; p. 34 © keith morris/Alamy Stock Photo; p. 37 AP Photo/Muskogee Phoenix, Jennifer Lyles; p. 38 © Tampa Bay Times/ZUMAPRESS.com; pp. 40–41 Photo by Stuart Ramson/Invision for Disney Consumer Products/AP Images; p. 44 © iStockphoto.com/Vonkara1; p. 46 White House Photo/Alamy Stock Photo; p. 48 Pamela Moore/E+/Getty Images; p. 50 Lucia Lambriex/Taxi/Getty Images; p. 52 Maciej Frolow/The Image Bank/Getty Images; interior pages checklist icon D Line/Shutterstock.com; back cover background photo Rawpixel.com/Shutterstock.com.

Designer: Michael Moy; Editor: Kathy Kuhtz Campbell;
Photo Researcher: Karen Huang